10/.

AARON RODGERS

SUPERSTAR QUARTERBACK

BIG BUDDY

NFL SUPERSTARS

Big Buddy Books
An Imprint of Abdo Publishing
abdobooks.com

DENNIS ST. SAUVER

abdobooks.com

Published by Abdo Publishing, a division of ABDO, PO Box 398166, Minneapolis, Minnesota 55439.
Copyright © 2020 by Abdo Consulting Group, Inc. International copyrights reserved in all countries.
No part of this book may be reproduced in any form without written permission from the publisher.
Big Buddy Books™ is a trademark and logo of Abdo Publishing.

Printed in the United States of America, North Mankato, Minnesota.
052019
092019

THIS BOOK CONTAINS
RECYCLED MATERIALS

Cover Photo: Dylan Buell/Getty Images; efks/Getty Images.
Interior Photos: Chris Trotman/Getty Images (p. 13); Darron Cummings/AP Images (p. 11); David
    Zalubowski/AP Images (p. 9); Grant Halverson/Getty Images (p. 5); Isaac Brekken/Getty Images
    (p. 23); Kevin Winter/Getty Images (p. 27); Leon Halip/Getty Images (p. 17); Matt Ludtke/Getty
    Images (p. 21); Ronald Martinez/Getty Images (p. 15); Stacy Revere/Getty Images (p. 29);
    Streeter Lecka/Getty Images (p. 19); Ted S. Warren/AP Images (p. 25).

Coordinating Series Editor: Elizabeth Andrews
Graphic Design: Jenny Christensen, Cody Laberda

Library of Congress Control Number: 2018967854

Publisher's Cataloging-in-Publication Data

Names: St. Sauver, Dennis, author.
Title: Aaron Rodgers: superstar quarterback / by Dennis St. Sauver
Other title: Superstar quarterback
Description: Minneapolis, Minnesota : Abdo Publishing, 2020 | Series: NFL superstars |
    Includes online resources and index.
Identifiers: ISBN 9781532119842 (lib. bdg.) | ISBN 9781532174605 (ebook)
Subjects: LCSH: Rodgers, Aaron, 1983- --Juvenile literature. | Football players--United
    States--Biography--Juvenile literature. | Quarterbacks (Football)--United States--Biography--
    Juvenile literature. | Green Bay Packers (Football team)--Juvenile literature.
Classification: DDC 796.3326409 [B]--dc23

CONTENTS

SUPERSTAR QUARTERBACK

Aaron Rodgers is a star quarterback in the National Football League (NFL). He plays for the Green Bay Packers in Wisconsin.

He is one of the best quarterbacks in the league. He holds many records for passing. After a ten-win season in 2010, Aaron led his team to a Super Bowl Championship.

SNAPSHOT

NAME:
Aaron Charles Rodgers

BIRTHDAY:
December 2, 1983

BIRTHPLACE:
Chico, California

POSITION:
Quarterback

COLLEGE TEAMS:
Butte College Roadrunners,
University of California,
Berkeley Golden Bears

CURRENT TEAM:
Green Bay Packers

EARLY YEARS

Aaron's parents are Edward and Darla. Edward played football in college, and Darla was a dancer. Aaron has two brothers, Jordan and Luke.

Aaron became a football fan when he was very young. He could watch an entire football game on TV when he was only two years old.

DID YOU KNOW?

By the time he was five years old, Aaron could throw a football through a hanging tire.

Where was Aaron Rodgers born?

STARTING OUT

Aaron attended Pleasant Valley High School in Chico, California. He played football and baseball. He was a shortstop and a pitcher for the baseball team.

He quickly became a star on the football team. In one game he scored six touchdowns. He also set a single-season record with 2,466 total yards (2,255 m) in 2001.

After watching Aaron play only one time, the University of California's head coach said, "that's the best quarterback I've ever seen. That kid will play in the NFL some day."

After spending a year at Butte College, Aaron earned a **scholarship** to attend the University of California, Berkeley. By the middle of his first year, he became the starting quarterback for the team. In 2003, he was named **Most Valuable Player (MVP)** of the Insight Bowl.

The next year, he led his team to a ten-win season. He earned a spot on the Pacific-10 All-**Conference** first team. He also tied an NCAA record for completing 23 straight **passes** in one game.

DID YOU KNOW?

Aaron's brother Jordan was on the TV show *The Bachelorette*.

When trying out for the NFL in 2005, Aaron ran the 40-yard (37 m) dash in 4.7 seconds!

BIG DREAMS

During college, Aaron thought about becoming a lawyer. But his love for football changed his mind. He wanted to be a professional in the NFL.

The Green Bay Packers drafted him in 2005. Aaron had to wait his turn to play as starting quarterback. The Packers already had a star quarterback named Brett Favre.

Aaron was drafted twenty-fourth overall in the 2005 NFL Draft. He was the second quarterback chosen that year.

GOING PRO

   After Brett Favre said he was going to retire in 2008, Aaron became the starting quarterback. He amazed everyone by passing for more than 4,000 yards (3,658 m) in his first year as a starter. He also threw for 28 touchdowns.

   The next year, he threw for 4,434 yards (4,054 m) and 30 touchdowns. In just two years, Aaron proved to be a valuable quarterback.

Aaron says that he remembers every touchdown and interception he has thrown since eighth grade.

The Packers have three rivals in the NFC North Division. Those teams are the Chicago Bears, Detroit Lions, and Minnesota Vikings.

From 2007 to 2018, Aaron played in 62 games against the three teams. Of those games, the Packers won 43 with Aaron's help.

In 2018, Aaron was the highest paid player in the NFL.

A RISING STAR

In October 2009, Aaron was named NFL Offensive Player of the Month. That month, he passed for 988 yards (903 m). He also completed almost 75 percent of his passes.

Aaron helped his team score 560 points in 2011. That was the second-highest scoring season in Packers history. For his efforts, Aaron earned AP MVP honors. And he was named the NFC Pro Bowl starting quarterback.

Aaron earned the NFL MVP Award for the 2011 and 2014 seasons.

Following the 2010 season, the Packers made it to the playoffs as a wild card team. Under Aaron's leadership, the team won the Super Bowl Championship!

The next season, Aaron led the Packers to 15 wins and only one loss. Sadly, the team was beat in the playoffs and did not make it back to the Super Bowl.

The Packers won the NFC North Division title in 2016. This completed a streak of eight straight years of making the playoffs.

On the day after winning the Super Bowl, 56,000 fans met the team to celebrate. The celebration was called Return to Titletown.

OFF THE FIELD

Aaron lives near Green Bay, Wisconsin, where the Packers team plays. He also owns a home in Del Mar, California.

In his spare time, Aaron loves to travel. In 2018, he went to India to help people who need hearing aids. He also enjoys acting. He has been in several State Farm Insurance commercials on TV.

When not on the football field, Aaron likes spending time on the golf course.

GIVING BACK

Aaron gives much of his time to special causes. He and his business partner David Gruber created the website itsAaron.com. It is an organization that supports people who are changing the world.

He is also a supporter of the Midwest Athletes Against Childhood Cancer (MACC) Fund. The group helps find cures for children who are sick.

Aaron received the Bart Starr Award for Character and Leadership in 2014.

AWARDS

The quarterback has won many awards. He has been selected to the **Pro Bowl** seven times. And he won the AP NFL **MVP** Award twice.

In 2012, Aaron was named number one of the NFL's Top 100 football players. He has also won six of ESPN's ESPY Awards while in the NFL. He won Best NFL Player four times.

Aaron also won ESPY Awards for Best Play in 2016 and 2017.

BUZZ

Aaron wants to continue playing with the Packers until he is at least 40 years old. After he retires, he would like to continue his philanthropy. He wants to help make the world a better place.

Aaron threw for 4,442 yards (4,062 m) during the 2018 season. It was the second-highest total of his career.

GLOSSARY

championship a game, a match, or a race held to find a first-place winner.

conference a group of sports teams that play against each other and that are part of a larger league of teams.

division a number of teams grouped together in a sport for competitive purposes.

draft a system for professional sports teams to choose new players.

Most Valuable Player (MVP) the player who contributes the most to his or her team's success.

organization (ohr-guh-nuh-ZAY-shuhn) a group of people united for a common purpose.

pass to throw the football in the direction of the opponent's goal.

philanthropy (fuh-LAN-thruh-pee) the desire and active effort to help other people.

playoffs a game or series of games to determine a championship or break a tie.

Pro Bowl a game that features the best players in the NFL. It does not count toward regular-season records.

professional (pruh-FEHSH-nuhl) paid to do a sport or activity.

retire to give up one's job.

rival one who competes for the same position as another.

scholarship (SKAH-luhr-ship) money or aid given to help a student continue his or her studies.

support to provide help or encouragement to.

title a first-place position in a contest.

valuable of great use or service.

ONLINE RESOURCES

Booklinks
NONFICTION NETWORK
FREE! ONLINE NONFICTION RESOURCES

To learn more about Aaron Rodgers, please visit **abdobooklinks.com** or scan this QR code. These links are routinely monitored and updated to provide the most current information available.

★ ★ ★ INDEX ★ ★ ★